1 MONTH OF FREE READING

at

www.ForgottenBooks.com

By purchasing this book you are eligible for one month membership to ForgottenBooks.com, giving you unlimited access to our entire collection of over 1,000,000 titles via our web site and mobile apps.

To claim your free month visit:

www.forgottenbooks.com/free28144

ISBN 978-0-365-42200-6
PIBN 10028144

For support please visit www.forgottenbooks.com

The Story of the Hurons

The
Story of the Hurons

BY

E. J. Hathaway

Printed for the Ontario Historical Society,
August, 1915

Reprinted from
Maclean's Magazine
August, 1915

The Story of the Hurons

THE beginnings of Canadian history are interwoven in the most intimate way with the efforts of the monarchy and nobility of France and the Church of Rome to graft upon the new world a system which in the old had brought corruption, strife, warfare and suffering. They formed a brilliant attempt to grasp half a continent, saddle it with the exactions of a feudal Government and stifle it with the burden of a grasping hierarchy.

Primarily the discovery of America by Columbus, the venturesome voyages of Cartier, the energetic exploits of Champlain, the hazardous journeyings to the far West of Joliet, LaSalle and others were due to the lure of the distant East—the desire to find a short way to the Kingdom of Cathay and secure access to its fabulous wealth. Secondary only to this were the claims of colonization, the founding of a new empire, the desire for trade with the Indians.

For many years following the explorations of Cartier in the new world, France had little chance to take advantage of the opportunities opened up, and it was not until the beginning of the seventeenth century that the spirit of commercial enterprise and the zeal for discovery awoke and any real effort was made to develop trade or encourage settlement.

An unsuccessful attempt was made in 1600 to establish a settlement at Tadoussac at the mouth of the Saguenay River, in order to secure control of the fur trade. A few years later another was founded by DeMonts and Champlain at Port Royal in Nova Scotia. The existence of Port Royal was for some years of the most precarious character. The severity of the climate, the jealousy of rival merchants, the constant disputes between French and English as to sovereignty—these were all discouraging elements.

Meanwhile Champlain in 1608 founded Quebec at one of the places visited by Cartier seventy years before. Champlain,

SAMUEL DE CHAMPLAIN,

Founded Quebec, 1608. Visited Algonquin
Indian Village on Ottawa River, 1613,
and arrived at Huron Country,
in present County of Simcoe,
August 1st, 1615.

however, had ambitions beyond that of trading furs. From the Algonquins who came to Quebec to trade he learned of lakes and rivers beyond the rapids and he cherished the hope that by tracing back the interior waters to their source a western route to China, Japan and India might be discovered. His other great desires were to establish the power of France and to plant the Catholic faith in the wilderness of the new world.

The first winter in Quebec was severe enough to test the endurance of the most courageous. The little band of twenty-eight that remained with Champlain was reduced to eight by the following May. With the return of the supply boat from France in the spring, the way was open for exploration and discovery. An agreement entered into between Champlain and the chief of the Algonquins to assist them against their enemies, the Iroquois—a federation of five powerful nations living in fortified villages within the present State of New York—resulted in the discovery of the Richelieu River and the lake that bears the name of the great French leader. By thus joining forces with the

Hurons and Algonquins Champlain hoped to open the way to the discovery of territory otherwise inaccessible; and while he gained the antagonism of the Iroquois, he at the same time became indispensable to his allies, and at the close of the first expedition readily accepted their invitation to visit their towns and to aid them further in their wars.

In 1610 Henry Hudson, in an effort to find a north-west passage to the Far East, had discovered Hudson Bay. Shortly afterward one of Champlain's young men, Nicolas de Vignau, was sent to spend a season with the Algonquins in their country up the Ottawa. On his return he told a marvelous tale of finding a great lake at the source of the Ottawa, from which another river flowed northward leading to the sea. Upon the shores of the sea he claimed to have seen the wreck of an English ship, evidently that of Hudson, whose crew had mutinied. This sea was said to be but seventeen days distant by canoe from Montreal.

This direct confirmation of his theory of a shortcut to the Pacific was so

important that early in the summer of
1613 Champlain set out to follow up the
discovery, taking Vignau with him. They
left St. Helen's Island, opposite Montreal,
on May 27th. Never before had a party
of white men penetrated this virgin country. The Ottawa, though navigable for
much of the way, has many swift currents,
tortuous passages and treacherous rapids.
Day after day they toiled on, paddling in
the clear currents, and pushing, dragging
or lifting their canoes across the difficult
places. They shouldered their boats
through the dense woods around the more
dangerous rapids, launching them again
in the more quiet waters, and at night
they made their camp on the edge of the
woody banks. Not only had they the
hardships of travel, but they suffered
much from pests of mosquitoes by day and
dangers from wild animals by night.

When they reached the Algonquin country the Indians told Champlain that the
rapids in the river above were impassable,
and Champlain was forced to accompany
them to the headquarters of the tribe on
Allumette Island.

Champlain begged the chiefs to furnish him with canoes and men to take him to the country of the Nipissings on Lake Nipissing, some distance further north. The request, at first granted, was afterwards denied. The rapids and rocks in the river were dangerous, and the wickedness of the Nipissings was inexpressible.

Champlain urged his claims with all his skill. The young man Vignau had been there; here was his story and a map showing the route he had taken.

The Indians were indignant. Vignau had spent the winter in their lodges. He had not been a mile farther north than they were at that moment. His story was a fabrication, his map an imposture. This proved to be the case. His desire for notoriety had been his undoing; and he had hoped that the difficulties of the journey and the dangers of the trip would have discouraged Champlain, and caused him to return without discovering his falsehood. There was now no good reason for continuing the expedition, and Champlain retraced his steps to Montreal.

Two years later, having spent the intervening period in France, Champlain re-

FATHER BRÉBEUF,

Jesuit Missionary. Arrived in Canada, 1626.
Killed by Iroquois in Massacre of Village of
St. Louis, present County of Simcoe,
March 16th, 1649.

turned again to Canada. He was accompanied this time by four Récollet priests, members of the Franciscan Order, for the purpose of ministering to the spiritual needs of the Indian population as well as to those of the French traders and settlers. They arrived at Quebec at the end of May, 1615, where, after choosing a site for their convent near the fortifications erected by Champlain, they built an altar, and on June 24th Father Dolbeau celebrated the first mass ever said in Canada. The congregation knelt on the bare earth, while the guns from the fort and from the ship in the river marked the occasion as one of special importance.

Father Jamay and Du Plesis were assigned to work at Quebec, Father Le Caron to establish a mission to the Hurons at their headquarters on Lake Huron, and Father Dolbeau to work among the Montagnais Indians on the St. Lawrence. Le Caron immediately set off to Montreal, then thronged with Indians on their annual visit for the trading of furs. The assembled Hurons and Algonquins also were eager for Champlain's assistance against the Iroquois. "With French

soldiers to fight their battles," says Parkman, "French priests to baptize them, and
French traders to supply their increasing
wants, their dependence would be complete." This was the policy of Champlain.
The Hurons and Algonquins agreed to
supply twenty-five hundred warriors; he
would join them with all the men at his
command; and a vigorous warfare would
be opened against the powerful Iroquois.
He returned to Quebec to make prepara-
tions for the expedition, and on his return
he found that Le Caron, with twelve
Frenchmen, had left with the Indians on
July the first for the Huron country.
Champlain, with two others and a party
of Hurons, set out eight days later.

Their way as far as the Algonquin village was by the course taken two years
before. From this point he advanced until
he reached the tributary waters at Matta-
wa, leading to Lake Nipissing. An outlet
at the western end of the lake led into the
French River, which carried them to the
great fresh-water sea of the Hurons, now
known as Georgian Bay. Their course for
more than a hundred miles continued
south along the eastern shore of Georgian

Bay, through the thirty thousand islands, to Thunder Bay at the entrance to Matchedash Bay near the harbor of Penetanguishene.

Champlain arrived in the Huron country on August 1st. On August 3rd he visited Carhagouha, a town surrounded by a triple palisade thirty-five feet high, where he found Le Caron engaged with the Indians in the erection of an altar.

Parkman thus describes the first religious ceremony ever held in the province of Ontario:

"The twelfth of August, 1615, was a day evermore marked with white in the friar's calendar. Arrayed in priestly vestments, he stood before his simple altar, behind him his little band of Christians— the twelve Frenchmen who had attended him and the two who had followed Champlain. Here stood their devout and valiant chief, and at his side that pioneer of pioneers, Etienne Brule, the interpreter. The Host was raised aloft; the worshippers kneeled. Then their rough voices joined in the hymn of praise, *Te Deum Laudamus;* and then a volley of their guns proclaimed the triumph of the *okies,* the *manitous*, and all the brood of anomalous devils who reigned with undisputed sway in these wild realms of darkness. The brave friar, a true soldier of the Church, had led his forlorn hope into the fastnesses of hell; and now, with contented heart, he might depart in peace, for he had said the first mass in the country of the Hurons."

The Hurons at the time of Champlain's visit occupied the district on the southeastern shore of Georgian Bay, lying between Matchedash Bay, Nottawasaga Bay, Lake Simcoe and Lake Couchiching. They were a numerous and powerful people, second only to the Iroquois in strength, in numbers and in methods of organization and government. They lived in villages and towns, many of them strongly fortified, and as early French writers estimate the population variously, it is inferred that migrations took place from time to time. Champlain estimates the number of villages as seventeen or eighteen, with the population at about ten thousand; but Brébeuf, twenty years later, found twenty villages and about 30,000 souls. In 1639 the Jesuit estimate is thirty-two inhabited villages and thirty-two thousand of a population. From this it will be seen that the number of people in the district at that time was as large as at the present time, including the large towns of Orillia, Midland and Penetanguishene.

Unlike most of the other Indian tribes, the Hurons were farmers, fishermen and traders, cultivating the land and raising corn, beans and other crops for food, and hemp for fishing lines and nets. From other nations they obtained, by barter, supplies of furs, tobacco and other merchantable goods, which they traded in the East for such other articles as they required.

The country of the Hurons is one of the most interesting archæological fields in Canada, and traces have been found of upwards of four hundred places, which beyond doubt, were the sites of Huron villages. The large number of places identified as village sites by reason of the ashes, debris, implements, fragments of pottery and other evidences of occupation, is accounted for in several ways. The domestic conditions under which they lived made it impossible to remain long in any one place; the land under cultivation, owing to the fact that repeated crops were taken from the same soil, soon became barren; the fuel supply gave out; the encroachments and harassments of the hostile Iroquois rendered a location untenable; any or all of these might at one time or another make it necessary to move from one place to another.

Most of the villages were situated in elevated places, because of their greater strategic value, and those on the southern and eastern fronts were strongly fortified by palisades as protection against invasion.

To the west of the Huron country was the country of the Petuns, called the Tobacco Nation, because they made a special feature of tobacco growing. In Southern Ontario from the Niagara to the Detroit River were the Neuters or Neutrals, so called because in the long conflicts between the Iroquois and the Hurons they remained aloof and took no part with one side or the other.

Champlain remained in the Huron country until September 1st, when the war party, now completed, set out on the expedition against the Iroquois. Their way lay along Lake Simcoe, across the portage to Balsam Lake, and down the chain of waterways known as the Trent River route until they reached Lake Ontario.

They boldly set out across the lake, landing near the eastern end, where, after hiding their canoes, they struck inland in search of the Iroquois headquarters, which they reached on October tenth. The enemy occupied a strongly fortified town south of Lake Oneida, which they defended with much skill. After nearly a week of futile fighting, during which Champlain himself received an arrow in the knee and another in the leg, the invaders began their retreat, carrying the wounded with them. The Hurons had promised to furnish Champlain with guides to take him to Quebec, but as he had not brought them victory they one and all began to make excuses. Nothing therefore remained but that he must return and spend the winter with them.

They reached Cahiagué, near the present town of Orillia, two days before

Christmas, and here, with the exception of visits to neighboring tribes in what are now the counties of Simcoe, Grey, Bruce and Dufferin, and to the Nipissings in the north, he remained until the following May.

The Huron mission languished between 1617 and 1622, although Father Poullain visited the Nipissing country during the summer of 1619. Work was resumed in 1623, when Le Caron returned, accompanied by Brother Sagard, the historian, and Father Viel. The first two returned to Quebec the following year, after having compiled a dictionary of the Huron language, and Father Viel was drowned on his way east a season later.

The Récollet mission in Canada was supplemented in 1626 by the arrival of a company of Jesuit priests, among whom were Lalemant and Brébeuf. Eighteen years had elapsed since the founding of Quebec, and its population was but one hundred and five, including men, women and children. Brébeuf, with two others, set out in company with the returning Indians soon after his arrival, and reached the Huron country in August,

FATHER LALEMANT,

Jesuit Missionary.   Arrived in Canada, 1626.
Killed by Iroquois in Massacre of Village of
St. Louis, present County of Simcoe
March 16th, 1649.

where he continued the work of the mission for three years.

After the taking of Quebec by Admiral Kirke in 1629 Canada remained in possession of the English until it was ceded back to France in 1632. During this time there were no missionaries in Ontario. The next missionary period began in 1634.

The history of the Jesuit mission to the Hurons during the next fifteen years is one of the most thrilling chapters in Canadian history. During these years upwards of twenty-five missionaries were engaged in the work, and at least five of them suffered martyrdom. From village to village they went, teaching, preaching and baptising in the name of Him whom they served. After a few years they established a headquarters of their own a little to the east of Penetanguishene, where they erected a chapel, mission house and hospital, surrounding them with a stone wall and a wooden barricade. From this centre, which they called Ste. Marie, they conducted missionary operations not only among the Hurons but also among the Petuns and the Neutrals.

But during all the years of the Huron mission there was the constant Iroquois menace. The French traded with the Hurons and Algonquins, and the Iroquois with the Dutch, by whom they had been supplied with brandy and firearms. Champlain's alliance with the Hurons and his expedition to the Iroquois country had but intensified the enmity. Communication with Quebec could only be made by the circuitous course of the French River and the Ottawa, because of the dangers of ambush and attack. When the Huron trading parties were strong, the Iroquois harassed their trail and raided their camps; when the latter were the stronger, the Hurons were massacred on the spot or captured and reserved for torture.

The finest hunting grounds for beaver lay to the north and west of the Great Lakes, and were largely in the hands of the Hurons, who carried their peltries only to the French at Montreal and Three Rivers. The Iroquois, jealous of their rivals in the north, determined to secure this trade for themselves. In order to accomplish it, the tribes which stood in their way must be destroyed, the Ottawa route closed, and the trade diverted from the French settlements to those of the Dutch and the English on the Hudson.

The first blow in this desperate campaign, which seems to have been planned with cunning, skill and daring, was struck in 1642, when Contarea, a fortified frontier village in the Huron country, five miles south-west of the present town of Orillia, was captured and its entire population either killed or taken captive. In 1648 the Iroquois returned and took the village of St. Joseph II., destroying it by fire and taking as prisoners some seven hundred of its people who were unable to escape. Father Daniel, the first of the missionaries to suffer death at their hands, was shot as he stood at mass, robed in surplice and stole, and every savage had a hand in mutilating his body.

These successes inspired the invaders to further conquests. They established a strategic base to the east of Lake Simcoe, crossing into the Huron country at the Narrows. On March 16th, 1649, the village of St. Ignace was attacked and destroyed, only two of the villagers escaping either death or capture. A few hours later the village of St. Louis was entered, and after setting it on fire the Iroquois returned to St. Ignace taking with them Father Brébeuf and Father Lalemant to be tortured. The terrible treatment of these two missionaries at the hands of the barbarous Iroquois is one of the most dreadful tales in the pages of our history. Brébeuf, though of stronger constitution, succumbed after four hours of torture, while Lalemant, of less rugged build, survived until the following day. Their charred and mangled bodies were found after the retreat of the Iroquois.

When news of the massacre reached the Christian Hurons in the village of Ossossane on the following day, a party of warriors engaged the Iroquois, and an obstinate struggle took place near and within the palisades of St. Louis, which had remained intact when the village was burned. By sheer weight of numbers the Hurons were overcome and destroyed, although the invaders lost heavily in the battle.

A day or two later the Iroquois set out hurriedly for home, laden with spoils and with prisoners, leaving the Huron rem-

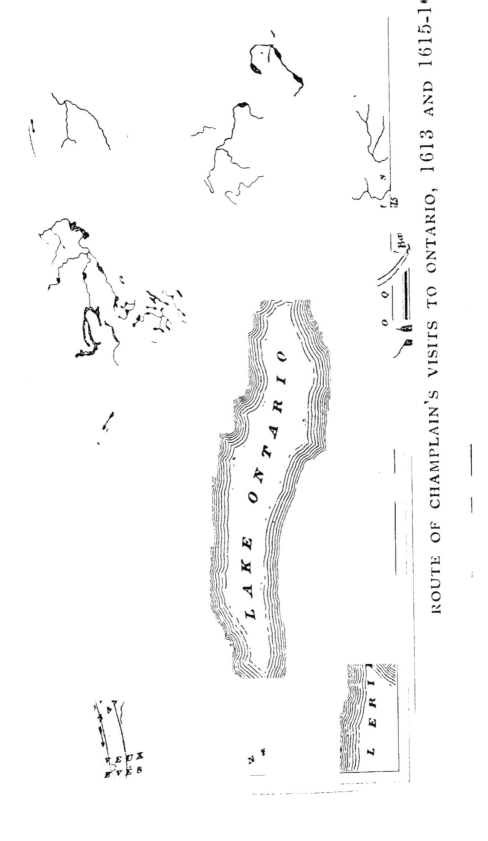

ROUTE OF CHAMPLAIN'S VISITS TO ONTARIO, 1613 AND 1615-1

nants in a panic of despair. The country soon became a vast expanse of smouldering ruins; village after village was destroyed and then abandoned, lest something of value should fall into the hands of the dreaded Iroquois. The panic spread from lodge to lodge, the people scattering whither they could. Some found their way across the ice on Nottawasaga Bay to the country of the Petuns, others sought shelter in the Blue Mountains, while others in the hope of finding safety removed to what is now known as Christian Island, a short distance from the mainland. Here also the Jesuit missionaries decided to establish their mission and make their headquarters.

In December of the same year the Iroquois, flushed with their success of the previous spring, returned to complete their work of conquest. Their attention this time was directed to the Petuns, and once again desolation and despair followed their visitation. It was not warfare, but butchery, and two more brave missionaries, Father Garnier and Father Chabanel, are sent to join the noble army of martyrs.

THE STORY OF THE HURONS.

Having destroyed the villages and lodges and practically all the warriors of the Hurons and Petuns, the Iroquois next turned to the Neutrals, their own neighbors to the west of the Niagara River. The events of the fall and winter of 1650 and 1651 were, if anything, more dreadful than those of the previous year. The slaughter was terrible, especially among the aged and very young. The men were not a fighting race, nor were they expert canoemen, and they proved no match for the huge invading bands from New York State. The number of prisoners was unusually large, and consisted mainly of young men and women, who were taken back to the Iroquois camp, where they became merged with the Seneca nation.

Within ten short years one of the greatest national tragedies in the human race had been enacted—three native races had been practically exterminated, and the whole country between Lake Erie and the Georgian Bay depopulated. A few only had escaped, and of their descendants but a few small bands now remain. At Lorette, near the city of Quebec, is a small reserve consisting of about five hundred persons, the descendants of those who escaped to Christian Island. Owing to their isolation and to the harassments of the ubiquitous Iroquois, they had been compelled to leave their refuge, and, accompanied by the French missionaries, they made their way as best they could to the shelter of Quebec. Another band, after much wandering in the West, returned, towards the end of the seventeenth century, to the Detroit River, and formed three settlements, one on the east bank at the present town of Sandwich, another on the western bank of the river, and a third on the south shore of Lake Erie near Sandusky. Another band occupies a small tract of land in a corner of the Indian Territory in the United States.

The story of the visit of Champlain in 1615 followed by the Jesuit mission to the Huron country from 1626 to 1650 is the complete first chapter in the history of Ontario. No effort was made at the time towards development or settlement, and it is probable that there were never more than sixty Europeans in the Huron country at any one time connected with the Indian missions, although the traders and trappers throughout Ontario associated with the French settlements and trading posts in the province of Quebec may have been numerous.

For many years following the dispersion of the Hurons the known history of the province of Ontario is singularly slender. The old trade route up the Ottawa and across the French River to the Georgian Bay was doubtless used to some extent in defiance of the Iroquois menace, although at a later date it gave way to the less arduous trip across from Lake Ontario to Georgian Bay. A mission was established at Quinte on Lake Ontario in 1666, and about the same time Marquette founded another at the Sault. Joliet had penetrated Western Ontario and had made an expedition under direction of Talon to explore the copper mines of Lake Superior. Father Hennepin visited the Humber River and Niagara Falls in 1678, and LaSalle two years later crossed from Lake Ontario to Georgian Bay by way of the Humber and Lake Simcoe. But apart from such expeditions and the visits of traders, the province of Ontario had no well defined history until well on in the eighteenth century. The story, however, of its discovery in the search for the North-West passage, of the visit of the great Champlain, of the founding of a mission among the native races then in occupation, and the tragic ending not only to the mission but also to the Indian nation itself, are among the notable events in our history.